JOSH ALLEN

DEREK MOON

WWW.APEXEDITIONS.COM

Apex is distributed by North Star Editions:
sales@northstareditions.com | 888-417-0195

Produced for Apex by Red Line Editorial.

Photographs ©: Doug Murray/AP Images, cover, 1; Joe Robbins/AP Images, 4–5, 58–59; Bryan M. Bennett/Getty Images Sport/Getty Images, 6–7, 50–51; Shutterstock Images, 8–9, 10–11, 18–19; Ben Jared/PGA Tour/Getty Images, 12–13; Justin Sullivan/Getty Images News/Getty Images, 14–15; Bobak Ha'Eri/Wikimedia Commons, 16–17; Ethan Miller/Getty Images Sport/Getty Images, 20–21; Matthew Holst/Getty Images Sport/Getty Images, 22–23; Loren Orr/Getty Images Sport/Getty Images, 24–25; Ric Tapia/AP Images, 26–27; Hannah Foslien/Getty Images Sport/Getty Images, 28–29; Jeff Zelevansky/Getty Images Sport/Getty Images, 30–31; Ralph Freso/Getty Images Sport/Getty Images, 32–33; Jeffrey T. Barnes/AP Images, 34–35; Michael Reaves/Getty Images Sport/Getty Images, 37; Jamie Squire/Getty Images Sport/Getty Images, 38–39, 40–41; Timothy T. Ludwig/Getty Images Sport/Getty Images, 42–43, 46–47, 49; Perry Knotts/Getty Images Sport/Getty Images, 44–45; Harry How/Getty Images Sport/Getty Images, 52–53; Ben Swanson/Denver Broncos/AP Images, 54–55; Brooke Sutton/Getty Images Sport/Getty Images, 56–57

Library of Congress Control Number: 2024952000

ISBN
979-8-89250-720-2 (hardcover)
979-8-89250-772-1 (paperback)
979-8-89250-754-7 (ebook pdf)
979-8-89250-738-7 (hosted ebook)

Printed in the United States of America
Mankato, MN
082025

NOTE TO PARENTS AND EDUCATORS

Apex books are designed to build literacy skills in striving readers. Exciting, high-interest content attracts and holds readers' attention. The text is carefully leveled to allow students to achieve success quickly.

TABLE OF CONTENTS

CHAPTER 1
UNSTOPPABLE 4

CHAPTER 2
SMALL-TOWN STAR 8

CHAPTER 3
COLLEGE CAREER 16

CHAPTER 4
GOING PRO 26

IN THE SPOTLIGHT
DOWNING THE DOLPHINS 36

CHAPTER 5
TIME TO SHINE 38

IN THE SPOTLIGHT
NEARLY PERFECT 48

CHAPTER 6
NFL STAR 50

TIMELINE • 58
COMPREHENSION QUESTIONS • 60
GLOSSARY • 62
TO LEARN MORE • 63
ABOUT THE AUTHOR • 63
INDEX • 64

CHAPTER 1

UNSTOPPABLE

The Buffalo Bills led the Kansas City Chiefs. But Buffalo faced a fourth down. Quarterback Josh Allen needed to get two yards. He lined up in the shotgun formation. Soon, Buffalo's center snapped the ball.

The Buffalo Bills faced the Kansas City Chiefs on November 17, 2024.

Allen grabbed the snap. The Chiefs closed in. So, Allen faked a pass. Then he took off running. He slipped past a defender to get the first down. But he didn't stop there. Three defenders bounced off Allen. No one could bring the quarterback down. He ran for a 26-yard touchdown. It sealed a Buffalo victory.

RIVAL QBs

Josh Allen and Patrick Mahomes are two of the NFL's best quarterbacks. So, meetings between the Bills and the Chiefs are often important. In 2024, Kansas City entered the game with a perfect 9–0 record. Allen and the Bills sent them home with their first loss.

Josh Allen finished the Chiefs game with 55 rushing yards.

CHAPTER 2

SMALL-TOWN STAR

Josh Allen was born in the small town of Firebaugh, California. He grew up with two sisters and a brother. Josh was the second of the four Allen children.

Firebaugh is in California's central valley.

Josh's family ran a large farm. There was lots of room to play. But Josh also had to help out. He took on many tasks. At an early age, he learned how to work hard.

FAMILY FARM

Josh's great-grandfather arrived in Firebaugh in the early 1900s. Josh's grandfather helped start the family farm. Later, Josh's dad and uncle took over.

The Allen family's farm grew cotton, cantaloupe, and other crops.

Growing up, Josh (left) and his brother (right) often played football together.

Josh is a year older than his brother, Jason. As kids, the two constantly competed. Both brothers were great athletes and played several sports. By high school, Josh stood 6-foot-3 (191 cm). He played quarterback for the football team. Josh had a strong arm. But the small-town star didn't get much attention from college coaches.

ALL-AROUND ATHLETE

Football was one of three sports Josh played in high school. He was the leading scorer on the basketball team. As a baseball pitcher, he could throw 90 miles per hour (145 km/h).

College coaches might have noticed Josh if he'd moved to a bigger school. But he stayed loyal to his hometown. Josh had a great senior season at Firebaugh High School. He threw for 33 touchdowns. However, Josh didn't get scholarship offers from any colleges. Instead, he decided to prove himself at a junior college.

Firebaugh is surrounded by farmland. Fewer than 10,000 people live in the town.

CHAPTER 3

COLLEGE CAREER

In 2014, Josh Allen joined the Reedley College football team. By the fifth game, he earned the starting quarterback job. Allen led the team in both passing and rushing. But he was ready for a bigger challenge.

Reedley College's mascot is a tiger.

Allen had excellent arm strength. He also had a growth spurt at Reedley. He grew to 6-foot-5 (196 cm). The extra size made him harder to tackle.

Allen emailed more than 1,000 college football coaches. But he got only a couple responses. Finally, two smaller schools offered him a scholarship. Allen decided to go to the University of Wyoming.

DREAM SCHOOL

Allen's first choice was to play for Fresno State. The school is only 40 miles (64 km) from Firebaugh. Allen grew up attending Fresno State games. However, the coach said Allen wasn't the right fit.

The University of Wyoming's football team plays at War Memorial Stadium.

Wyoming was not part of a power conference. And its football program hadn't seen much success. Even so, Allen was excited to make his mark. However, he broke his collarbone during his first start in 2015.

The next year went better. Allen showed off his passing skills. Wyoming even reached a bowl game. The team hadn't done that in five years. Allen's play caught the attention of NFL scouts.

Allen threw 28 touchdown passes in 2016.

In 2017, Allen led Wyoming to a record of 8–5.

After the 2016 season, Allen thought about entering the NFL Draft. But he decided to spend another year at Wyoming. He wanted to make sure he was fully prepared for the NFL. Allen led Wyoming to another successful season in 2017.

WHAT A FINISH

In 2017, Allen led Wyoming to a bowl game for the second year in a row. He showed that he could succeed when the stakes were high. Allen threw for three touchdowns. Wyoming won 37–14.

Allen had shown he was ready for the NFL. But the first six teams in the draft passed on the small-school star. Two other quarterbacks were picked ahead of him. Finally, the Buffalo Bills made a move. They traded up to get the seventh pick. Allen was headed to Buffalo.

DRAFT PROFILE

Scouts liked Allen's size and strength. They also liked his speed. However, his passes sometimes missed their targets. Also, Allen didn't have much experience playing against top teams. Scouts wondered how he would do against NFL defenses.

Allen completed only 56 percent of his passes in 2017.

CHAPTER 4

GOING PRO

Allen joined a struggling Buffalo Bills team. He began the 2018 season as the backup quarterback. But Buffalo's starter played poorly in Week 1. So, Allen came in to finish the game. It was a miserable 47–3 loss.

Allen threw for only 74 yards in his first NFL game.

The next game didn't go much better. Fans expected Week 3 to be a loss, too. Instead, Allen led a shocking 27–6 upset over the Minnesota Vikings. He scored on foot and through the air. The Bills struggled through the rest of the year. They finished with a 6–10 record. But Allen showed he could be a difference maker.

CAREER HIGH

Allen rushed for 135 yards in Week 13 of the 2018 season. The Bills fell to the Miami Dolphins that week. But it was a career-high rushing performance for the young star.

Allen threw for 196 yards in Week 3. He ran for another 39 yards.

Allen's skills helped the Bills go 10–6 in 2019. He could make big throws. But he also made mistakes. Sometimes, Allen missed easy passes. The quarterback's inconsistency showed in his first playoff game. Buffalo fell to the Houston Texans in overtime.

HARD HISTORY

The Bills have had an up-and-down history. In the early 1990s, they reached four straight Super Bowls. But they lost all four. From 2000 to 2016, the team had only two winning seasons.

Allen completed just 58.8 percent of his passes in 2019. That ranked among the lowest in the NFL.

In 2020, Allen set a Bills record with 37 touchdown passes.

COVID-19 spread around the world in 2020. Many events were canceled. Allen used the time to focus on his training. He came into the next season with better footwork. Suddenly, Allen was one of the league's best passers. His breakout season helped the Bills pile up 13 wins.

MR. BREAKFAST

In 2020, Allen teamed up with a company to create a new breakfast cereal. Fans ate up Josh's Jaqs. The cereal helped raise money for a children's hospital in Buffalo.

BILLS
17

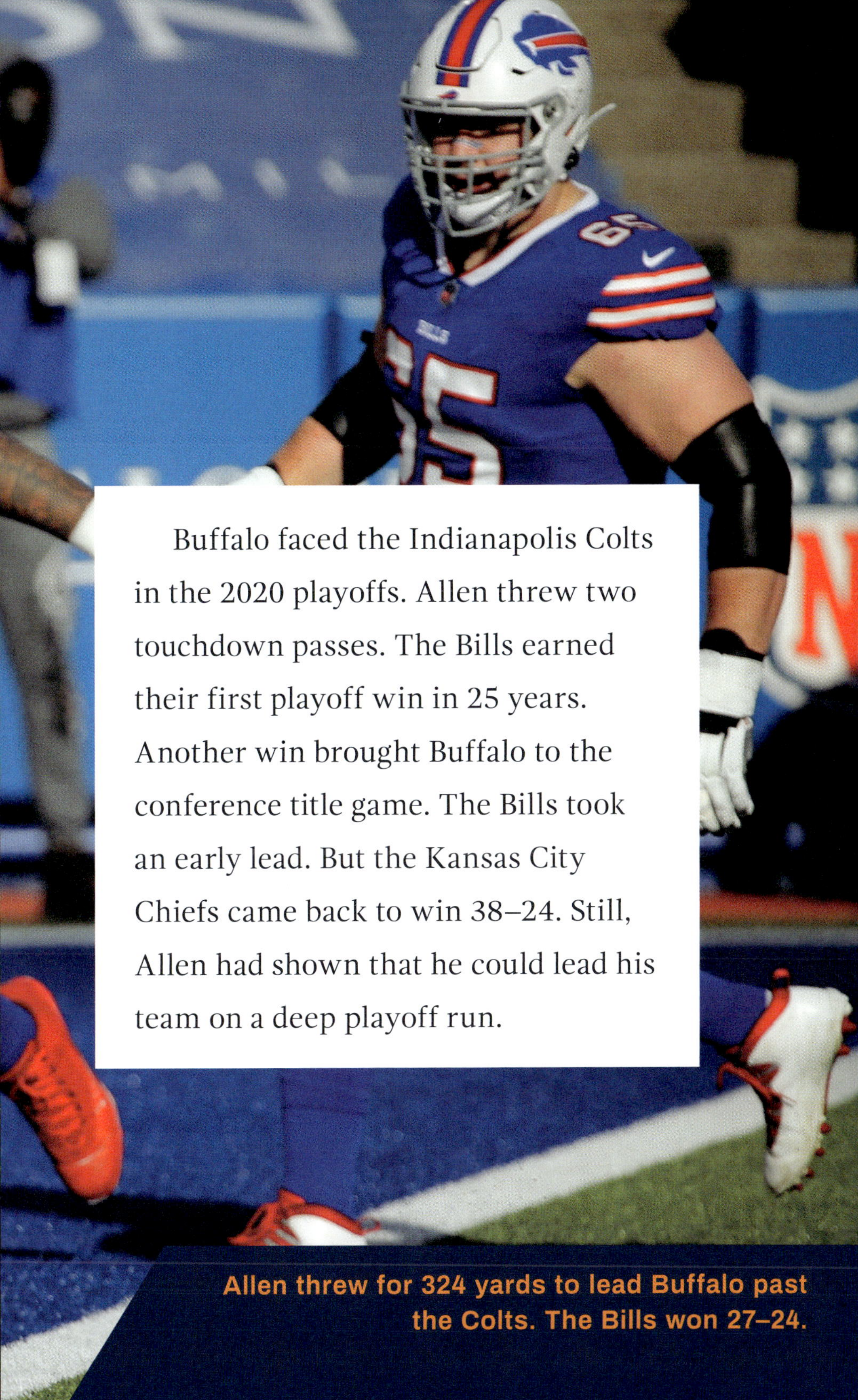

Buffalo faced the Indianapolis Colts in the 2020 playoffs. Allen threw two touchdown passes. The Bills earned their first playoff win in 25 years. Another win brought Buffalo to the conference title game. The Bills took an early lead. But the Kansas City Chiefs came back to win 38–24. Still, Allen had shown that he could lead his team on a deep playoff run.

Allen threw for 324 yards to lead Buffalo past the Colts. The Bills won 27–24.

IN THE SPOTLIGHT

DOWNING THE DOLPHINS

Josh Allen opened the 2020 season with a red-hot passing day. He played even better in Week 2. The Miami Dolphins stopped Buffalo's first drive. Then everything clicked for Allen. The quarterback led a long touchdown drive. He completed pass after pass.

Allen's second touchdown pass of the day came in the second quarter. Then, he threw two more touchdown passes in the fourth quarter. One of those was a 46-yard bomb. It gave Allen his first four-touchdown game. And Buffalo grabbed a 31–28 win.

ALLEN THREW FOR 415 YARDS AGAINST THE MIAMI DOLPHINS.

BILLS
17

CHAPTER 5

TIME TO SHINE

In August 2021, Allen signed a new contract to stay with the Bills for six more years. The Bills returned to Kansas City in Week 5. Allen made big plays all over the field. He led Buffalo past the rival Chiefs.

Allen threw for three touchdowns and ran for another against the Chiefs.

The Bills went on to win another division title. Then, Allen notched another win in the playoffs. That set up a rematch with the Chiefs. Allen was on fire. But so was Chiefs quarterback Patrick Mahomes. It was a back-and-forth game. However, Kansas City won 42–36 in overtime.

TOP TALENTS

In their postseason rematch, Allen and Mahomes both topped 300 passing yards. Neither quarterback threw an interception. And both ran for 65-plus yards.

Allen threw four touchdowns in Buffalo's overtime loss.

In 2022, Allen led the Bills to a third straight division title. Along the way, he passed for 424 yards in a Week 5 game. But once again, Buffalo was stopped short in the postseason. The Bills fell in their second playoff game. This time, the Cincinnati Bengals beat them 27–10.

GREAT GOLFER

Allen loves to play golf. In 2022, he competed in a tournament. Allen also played in a televised charity match. He had an unlikely teammate. Patrick Mahomes joined Allen to compete against two other top quarterbacks.

Allen threw for three touchdowns in a playoff win over the Miami Dolphins.

Allen struggled in the first part of the 2023 season. After a 5–5 start, the Bills fired their offensive coordinator. Things changed after that. Buffalo began running the ball more. Defenses didn't know what to expect. This made Allen more dangerous. The Bills ended the season with a five-game winning streak.

LEAGUE LEADER

Allen had 44 total touchdowns in 2023. That led the league. He also led the league with 4,830 total yards of offense.

Allen scored 15 rushing touchdowns during the 2023 season.

Heavy snow delayed Buffalo's 2023 playoff opener against the Pittsburgh Steelers. Allen wasn't bothered, though. He threw three touchdown passes. He also ran 52 yards for another score. The Bills won 31–17. Kansas City came to town the next week. Allen played well. But once again, the Bills fell in their second playoff game.

In Buffalo's win over the Steelers, Allen had 203 passing yards and 74 rushing yards.

IN THE SPOTLIGHT

NEARLY PERFECT

Allen's speed and power kept defenses on edge. That gave him time to burn opponents with his passing. On January 15, 2022, the New England Patriots found that out the hard way.

The two teams met in the playoffs. Allen was nearly perfect. He led Buffalo's offense down the field again and again. The Bills scored on all seven offensive possessions. No team in the Super Bowl era had done that before. Buffalo won the game 47–17.

ALLEN THREW FIVE TOUCHDOWN PASSES AGAINST THE PATRIOTS.

CHAPTER 6

NFL STAR

The Bills lost some key players in 2024. Allen knew he had to step up. He worked on being a better leader. Teammates fed off his hard work.

The Bills started the 2024 season with three straight wins.

Allen kept Buffalo competitive all season. The quarterback did it all during a snowy game in December. First, he threw for a touchdown. Later, he caught a touchdown pass during a trick play. Then he ran for another touchdown. Allen became the first NFL quarterback with a passing, rushing, and receiving touchdown in the same game.

MORE HISTORY

The Bills played the Los Angeles Rams on December 8, 2024. Allen threw for three touchdowns. He ran for three more. That hadn't been done since 1954.

Allen racked up 342 passing yards and 82 rushing yards against the Rams.

The Bills finished the 2024 season with a 13–4 record. Allen kept up his great play in the postseason. First, the Bills crushed the Denver Broncos 31–7. Then, Buffalo faced the Baltimore Ravens. It was a cold, snowy day. But Allen kept the ball safe. He led the Bills to a 27–25 win.

Allen threw for two touchdowns in a playoff win over the Broncos.

The conference championship game was a rematch against the Chiefs. Allen capped off the first half with a 34-yard touchdown pass. In the fourth quarter, he led a game-tying drive. However, Kansas City won with a late field goal. Buffalo fell short once again. But Bills fans hoped it wouldn't be long before Allen led the team to the Super Bowl.

TOP PLAYER

Despite losing key receivers, Allen had 28 passing touchdowns in 2024. He added another 12 scores on the run. After the season, Allen won his first Most Valuable Player (MVP) award.

Allen dives over defenders for a first down.

TIMELINE

1996 — On May 21, Josh Allen is born in Firebaugh, California.

2013 — As a senior in high school, Josh throws for 33 touchdowns.

2014 — Allen becomes the starting quarterback for Reedley College.

2017 — Allen leads Wyoming to a win at the Famous Idaho Potato Bowl.

2018 — The Buffalo Bills trade up to select Allen seventh in the NFL Draft.

2020	2022	2024	2025
Allen leads the Bills to their first division title in 25 years.	On January 15, Allen throws for five touchdowns to beat the New England Patriots in the playoffs.	On December 5, Allen becomes the first NFL quarterback to score a passing, rushing, and receiving touchdown in the same game.	Allen is named the NFL's Most Valuable Player (MVP).

COMPREHENSION QUESTIONS

Write your answers on a separate piece of paper.

1. Write a paragraph that explains the main ideas of Chapter 4.
2. Which of Josh Allen's stats do you think is most impressive? Why?
3. Against which team did Allen get his first NFL win?
   A. Miami Dolphins
   B. Minnesota Vikings
   C. New England Patriots
4. How much did Buffalo's record improve between Allen's first and second seasons?
   A. four wins
   B. five wins
   C. six wins

5. What does **loyal** mean in this book?

College coaches might have noticed Josh if he'd moved to a bigger school. But he stayed ***loyal*** *to his hometown. Josh had a great senior season at Firebaugh High School.*

A. faithful
B. unfriendly
C. disconnected

6. What does **inconsistency** mean in this book?

He could make big throws. But he also made mistakes. Sometimes, Allen missed easy passes. The quarterback's ***inconsistency*** *showed in his first playoff game.*

A. when a player is fast and strong
B. when a player is always the same
C. when a player is not dependable

Answer key on page 64.

GLOSSARY

bowl game
A postseason college football game that successful teams are invited to take part in.

conference
A group of teams that make up part of a sports league.

coordinator
An assistant coach who is in charge of the offense, defense, or special teams.

division
In the NFL, a group of teams that make up part of a conference.

draft
A system that lets teams select new players coming into the league.

overtime
An extra period that happens if two teams are tied at the end of the fourth quarter.

possessions
Times when a team has control of the ball and tries to score.

power conference
A high-level college conference, typically made up of large, successful schools.

scholarship
Money given to someone to help pay for college.

shotgun
A formation in which the quarterback begins the play about five yards behind the line of scrimmage.

TO LEARN MORE

BOOKS

Hewson, Anthony K. *Josh Allen*. Abdo Publishing, 2024.

Pettiford, Rebecca. *Josh Allen*. Bellwether Media, 2024.

Scheff, Matt. *Buffalo Bills*. Apex Editions, 2025.

ONLINE RESOURCES

Visit **www.apexeditions.com** to find links and resources related to this title.

ABOUT THE AUTHOR

Derek Moon is an author and avid Stratego player who lives in Watertown, Massachusetts, with his wife and daughter.

INDEX

Allen, Jason, 13

Baltimore Ravens, 54

Cincinnati Bengals, 42

Denver Broncos, 54

Firebaugh, California, 9, 11, 14, 18
Fresno State, 18

Houston Texans, 30

Indianapolis Colts, 35

Josh's Jaqs, 33

Kansas City Chiefs, 4, 6, 35, 39–40, 46, 56

Los Angeles Rams, 52

Mahomes, Patrick, 6, 40, 42
Miami Dolphins, 28, 36
Minnesota Vikings, 28
Most Valuable Player (MVP) award, 56

New England Patriots, 48
NFL Draft, 23–24

overtime, 30, 40

Pittsburgh Steelers, 46
playoffs, 30, 35, 40, 42, 46, 48, 54, 56

Reedley College, 17–18

Super Bowl, 30, 48, 56

University of Wyoming, 18, 20, 23

ANSWER KEY:

1. Answers will vary; 2. Answers will vary; 3. B; 4. A; 5. A; 6. C